The Moon

Written by Nadia Roberts

CELEBRATION PRESS
Pearson Learning Group

It's a beautiful night. The moon is full. It's a good time to look at the moon. Some people like to study the moon through a **telescope**.

Long ago, before there were telescopes,
people thought the moon was made of
cheese. Some people thought there was a
man in the moon. Others thought a
rabbit lived there.

Now we know that people and rabbits can't live on the moon. There is no air! The moon isn't made of cheese. It's rocky and dusty.

The moon is covered with mountains and **craters**. Telescopes help us see them. When the sun shines on them, their shadows may look like faces. But there are no real faces there.

Craters are made by **meteorites**. Meteorites are rocks that fly through space. Some land on the moon.

When these meteorites crash into the moon, they make holes. Some craters are over 300 miles wide! Others are only a half mile wide. Sometimes you can see little craters inside big craters.

Astronauts first visited the moon on July 20, 1969. Twelve astronauts visited the moon on six different trips between 1969 and 1972.

They left their footprints in the dust. One astronaut even hit a golf ball out into space! Maybe it's in orbit!

The moon doesn't make its own light. We see the moon because the sun shines on it.

Sun

Moon

Earth

The moonlight that lights our nights is really light reflected from the sun.

The moon moves around the earth. As it does, the shape of the moon seems to change.

Depending on where we are on Earth, we see the part of the moon that the sun lights up.

Full Moon

Half Moon

Crescent Moon

The moon is about 240,000 miles away from the earth. That's more than 80 trips across the United States!

Some scientists think that the moon may be made up of pieces of Earth. These pieces might have broken off millions of years ago. But no one is really sure where the moon came from.

Maybe you will visit the moon one day.
Maybe you will even leave your
footprints in the moon dust.

Glossary

astronaut   a person who goes into space

crater   a hole in the moon or in a planet that was made by a meteorite

meteorite   a space rock that crashes onto the moon or a planet

telescope   a tool people use to look at faraway things